A Note to Parents and Teachers

DK READERS is a compelling reading programme for children, designed in conjunction with leading literacy experts, including Cliff Moon M.Ed., Honorary Fellow of the University of Reading. Cliff Moon has spent many years as a teacher and teacher educator specializing in reading and has written more than 160 books for children and teachers. He is series editor to Collins Big Cat.

Beautiful illustrations and superb full-colour photographs combine with engaging, easy-to-read stories to offer a fresh approach to each subject in the series. Each DK READER is guaranteed to capture a child's interest while developing his or her reading skills, general knowledge, and love of reading.

The five levels of DK READERS are aimed at different reading abilities, enabling you to choose the books that are exactly right for your child:

Pre-level 1: Learning to read
Level 1: Beginning to read
Level 2: Beginning to read alone
Level 3: Reading alone
Level 4: Proficient readers

The "normal" age at which a child begins to read can be anywhere from three to eight years old. Adult participation through the lower levels is very helpful for providing encouragement, discussing storylines and sounding out unfamiliar words.

No matter which level you select, you can be sure that you are helping your child learn to read, then read to learn!

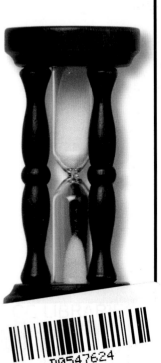

LONDON, NEW YORK, MUNICH,
MELBOURNE, AND DELHI

Series Editor Deborah Lock
Art Editor Sadie Thomas
DTP Designer Ben Hung
Production Georgina Hayworth
Picture Researcher Rob Nunn
Illustrator Peter Dennis

Reading Consultant
Cliff Moon, M.Ed.

Published in Great Britain by
Dorling Kindersley Limited
80 Strand, London WC2R ORL

Copyright © 2007 Dorling Kindersley Limited
A Penguin Company

2 4 6 8 10 9 7 5 3
DD392 - 04/07

A CIP catalogue record for this book
is available from the British Library

ISBN: 978-1-4053-2146-4

Colour reproduction by Colourscan, Singapore
Printed and bound in China by L Rex Printing Co., Ltd.

The publisher would like to thank the following for their kind
permission to reproduce their photographs.
a=above, b=below, c=centre, l=left, r=right, t=top.
Alamy Images: A Room With Views 6-7; Richard Levine 48br.
The Bridgeman Art Library: The Makins Collection 24. **Corbis:**
22br; Bettmann 26; Grace/zefa 4b. Hulton-Deutsch Collection
19tr; Wolfgang Kaehler 14; Markus Moellenberg/zefa 29t; Carl &
Ann Purcell 21bl; Tim Thompson 3cb, 20r; Holger Winkler/zefa
5c. **DK Images:** NASA 28bl, 28cb; National Maritime Museum,
London 2tr, 19tl; Natural History Museum, London 25tr; Stephen
Oliver 15tl, 30cr, 49br; The Science Museum, London 15tr, 18crb.
National Institute of Standards and Technology / NIST: Geoffrey
Wheeler Photography 28tr. **Science & Society Picture Library:**
Science Museum 13cr, 13cra, 13tr. **Science Photo Library:** 16tl.
SuperStock: Maria Ferrari 16-17.

All other images © Dorling Kindersley Limited
For more information see: www.dkimages.com

Discover more at
www.dk.com

DK READERS

BEGINNING TO READ ALONE
2

Telling the Time

Written by Patricia J. Murphy

A Dorling Kindersley Book

Do you know what time it is?

We tell the time many times a day.

When is football practice?

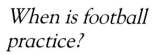

What time is dinner?

When does the party start?

What time will you get there?

We use clocks to tell the time.
They help people plan their day.
People have been telling the time
for a long, long *time!*

Clocks from long ago did not look
like ours and they did not keep
the best time either.
This is the story of how clocks
have changed.

Once upon a time, people woke up when the sun rose and went to bed when the moon and stars came out. These were the first clocks. Sometimes, people used stone pillars to mark the movement of the sun, moon and stars during the year.

Stonehenge in England

More than 5,500 years
ago, ancient Egyptians
watched shadows
to tell the time.
They placed sticks
called gnomons
in the ground.
They also built
stone pillars
called obelisks.

Obelisk

Timeline

Prehistoric times   3500 BCE

Telling the time with a gnomon

These sticks and obelisks cast
long shadows on the ground.
As the sun moved, the direction
of the shadows told people
what part of the day it was.
These were the very first sundials.

In 1500 BCE,
the Egyptians built
an even better
sundial.

Prehistoric times   3500 BCE   1500 BCE

It was shaped like a T and
had special markings.
The marks split the day into
ten hours of daylight and
two hours of twilight.
Like all sundials, this one could
only tell the time in sunlight.
People could not tell what time
it was on cloudy days or at night.

Time for bed, Tut!
Around 600 BCE,
Egyptians lined up two
tools called merkhets
with the stars to tell
the time at night.

Starting in 1400 BCE, ancient Egyptians and Greeks used water clocks to tell the time during the day and the night.

Timeline

Prehistoric times   3500 BCE   1500 BCE   1400 BCE

Water-clock tower
In 1088, Su Sung, a Chinese monk, built an amazing water-clock tower. It was more than 9 metres (30 feet) tall and had many moving parts.

Water was poured into a bowl with holes in it. As the water dripped out through the holes, people checked the water levels using special marks. This told them how much time had passed.

Water-level marks

Seven hundred years ago,
big and heavy
weight-driven clocks
were invented.
Many of these clocks
had round faces and
moving hands.
After the weights
were raised up,
they would lower
slowly to make
the clocks work.

Bells on this clock tower
rang on the hour.

Timeline

Prehistoric times   3500 BCE   1500 BCE   1400 BCE   1300

The outside and inside of a pocket watch

Two hundred years later, clocks were made that were powered by springs instead of weights. They were small and light, and some were made to fit in pockets. These tiny timepieces were the first pocket watches.

1500

In 1582, Galileo Galilei noticed that an oil lamp swinging from a chain kept perfect time. He found that a swinging weight always took the same number of beats to go backwards and forwards.

The cuckoo clock

This pendulum clock makes a whistle that sounds like a cuckoo bird every hour. If it is 12 o'clock, it whistles 12 times!

Another name for a swinging weight is a pendulum.

In 1657, Christiaan Huygens invented a clock that used a pendulum to keep time.

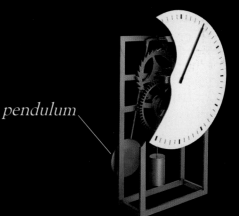

pendulum

On the high seas, sailors needed to know the exact time to find their way. Pendulum clocks needed to stand still and would not work on choppy waters.

Sands of time

Sometimes, sailors used hourglasses filled with sand or powdered eggshells to tell the time. The powder would take one hour to flow from the top to the bottom bulb.

Timeline

Prehistoric times   *3500 BCE*   *1500 BCE*   *1400 BCE*   *1300*

John Harrison

H4 chronometer

In 1759, John Harrison invented
the H4 chronometer, a special clock
to use on ships.
It worked so well that it won
a prize from the British government.

1500   *1657*   *1759*

Clocks had problems on land, too.
Each town set its clocks
using the sun.
When the sun reached
the highest place in
the sky, it was 12 noon
for that town.

Since the sun reaches the highest
place in the sky at different times
in different places, every town
had its own 12 noon!
Time was different
all over the place.
It was a mess!

1500   1657   1759

Many people thought it was silly
for every town to have its own time.
They asked questions like:
"How can railways and
mail coaches run on time?"
"How can people meet for lunch
or do business?"
"How can we fix this problem?"
Sandford Fleming, a railway
worker, knew the answer.

Greenwich Mean Time
Greenwich Mean Time (GMT)
is the time in Greenwich,
England. Each time zone was
described by how many hours
away from GMT it was.

Royal Observatory
Greenwich

Timeline

Prehistoric times   *3500 BCE*   *1500 BCE*   *1400 BCE*   *1300*

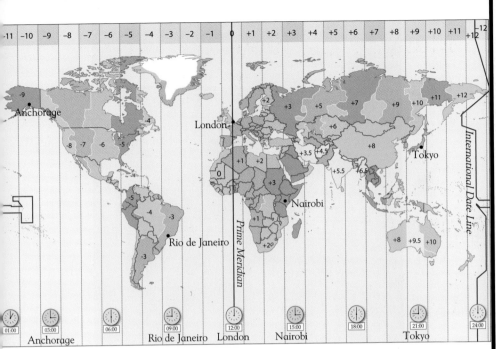

A map of the world's time zones

His idea was to divide
the world into 24 time zones.
Each zone was exactly one hour
apart from its neighbours.
Now, time was the same for
everyone in each zone.

1500   1657   1759   1884

In the 1880s, women were
the first to wear wristwatches.
After soldiers wore them in
World War I, men liked
to wear them as well.

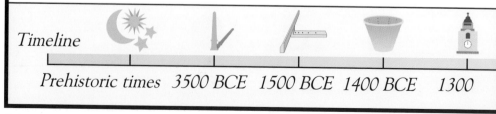

Timeline

Prehistoric times   3500 BCE   1500 BCE   1400 BCE   1300

Later, watches with tiny quartz crystals inside would become the best timekeepers. The crystals moved like pendulums, but kept even better time. Quartz watches are still popular today.

Quartz crystal

Quartz watch

Digital quartz watches

In 1972, quartz watches went digital. A display of numbers appeared instead of, or as well as, a clock face.

The first
atomic clock

NATIONAL BUREAU OF STANDARDS

Timeline

Prehistoric times   3500 BCE   1500 BCE   1400 BCE   1300

Quartz watches no longer keep
the most exact time.
What does?
Atomic clocks do!
Atomic clocks use atoms –
tiny particles, too small for us
to see – to help tell the time.
The atoms act like pendulums.
They move backwards and forwards
billions of times per second.
This lets atomic clocks tell the time
to a billionth of a second.

*Modern atomic
wristwatch*

1500   1657   1759   1884   1885   1949

Exact timekeeping

In 1999, scientists invented the world's most exact clock. It is called NIST-F1. It will not gain or lose a second in millions of years.

Space travel

So, why do we need to tell the time to a billionth of a second?

Satellites

Radio and television broadcasts

Many kinds of
technology that
we use today need
the split-second time
of an atomic clock
to work.
These pages show
just a few examples.

*Mobile
phones*

Today, clocks come in all shapes, sizes, colours and styles. Some flash, make sounds, play music or say the time out loud. Others time how fast you run.

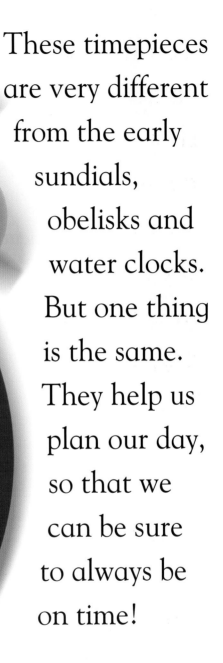

These timepieces
are very different
from the early
sundials,
obelisks and
water clocks.
But one thing
is the same.
They help us
plan our day,
so that we
can be sure
to always be
on time!

Timely facts

Long-case clocks were built
to hide their long pendulums.
The song "Grandfather's Clock"
written in 1876, inspired people
to call them grandfather clocks.

The ancient Egyptians were
the first people to divide the hour
into 60 parts, or minutes.
Their number system was based
on the number 60 and was easy
to divide by 2, 3, 4, 5 and 10.

The world's smallest clock is an
atomic clock the size of a grain
of rice created by the National
Institute for Standards and
Technology in Boulder,
Colorado, in 2004.

The Colgate Palmolive
clock is one of the world's
biggest clocks. It measures
16.8 metres (55 feet) around!
It stands in Jersey City,
New Jersey, and was built
in 1924.